FINANCIAL *forevermore* WORKBOOK

A COUPLE'S FINANCIAL SURVIVAL GUIDE

...and Ways to Beat the Odds

NINA NEEDLEMAN

Financial Forevermore
A Couple's Financial Survival Guide and Ways to Beat the Odds
Nina Needleman

Published by Personal Finance Whisperer, Saint Louis, MO

Project Management and Book Design: Davis Creative, LLC / CreativePublishingPartners.com

Publisher's Cataloging-in-Publication
(Provided by Cassidy Cataloguing Services, Inc.).

Names:	Needleman, Nina, author.
Title:	Financial forevermore workbook : a couple's financial survival guide ... and ways to beat the odds / Nina Needleman.
Description:	Saint Louis, MO : Personal Finance Whisperer, [2023]
Identifiers:	ISBN: 979-8-9892577-0-6 | LCCN: 2023922480
Subjects:	LCSH: Married people--Finance, Personal. | Finance, Personal. | Money. | Financial risk management. | BISAC: FAMILY & RELATIONSHIPS / Marriage & Long term Relationships. | BUSINESS & ECONOMICS / Personal Finance / Money Management. | BUSINESS & ECONOMICS / Finance / Financial Risk Management.
Classification:	LCC: HG179 .N44 2023 | DDC: 332.0240655--dc23

ACKNOWLEDGMENTS

My parents Phil and Sima Needleman, for providing the role model of a good marriage and good money habits;

My publishing team: Cathy Davis and Missy Asikainen, for their expertise and guidance on updating and upgrading the current version to be more relevant in today's dating world;

Thanks to Psychologist Larry Shapiro, owner of Quantum Behavioral LLC, for his feedback and suggestions;

My friends and network, for their support.

DISCLAIMER

PART ONE

GROUNDWORK FOR A GREAT MARRIAGE

Money is a singular thing. It ranks with love as man's greatest source of joy. And with death as his greatest source of anxiety. Over all history it has oppressed nearly all people in one of two ways: either it has been abundant and very unreliable, or reliable and very scarce.

— John Kenneth Galbraith[1]

Congratulations!

This is one of the most exciting times of your lives—a time to savor and enjoy! You're in love, you're engaged, and you're planning the big day!

While you may meet with your religious advisor to discuss your spiritual commitment and the sanctity of marriage, your commitment to each other is actually being made on many levels. You are committing physically, emotionally, spiritually, socially, and financially to each other. Five facets of commitment are like five facets of a star: Each part is critical to the success of the whole.

The financial part is the component of the total commitment that is most often neglected in the many stages of connecting two people together. All components are necessary to achieve a successful long-term union/marriage/life together. But it is the financial piece of the puzzle that people prepare for the least and can have a spiraling impact on the integrity of the "star" or union.

The goal of this book is to ensure you begin your marriage with open communication about money and the ability to set realistic goals.

There are many reasons couples don't discuss their financial challenges and a variety of problems the lack of discussion can cause:

- In many families, money is a taboo topic.
- People avoid discussing money.
- People avoid addressing money problems together.
- Sometimes one person is hiding an issue from the other.
- Sometimes one person is mismanaging finances or credit.
- Sometimes one person is embarrassed by his or her bad decisions, purchases, or problems.
- Sometimes a person is embarrassed by his or her family's money and debt history or a bankruptcy.
- Sometimes one person is in denial about outstanding debts and loans.
- Sometimes ego is involved.
- Sometimes unequal earnings and/or power in the relationship leads one person to make assumptions about the handling of money.
- Lack of money by one party or abundance by one party can cause tension.
- Some individuals define themselves by their money habits.
- Others use money to control another.

WHY THIS WORKBOOK IS IMPORTANT

According to census data, 50 percent of people entering first marriages get divorced. Fifty-seven percent of divorced couples in the United States cited financial problems as the primary reason for the demise of their marriage according to a survey conducted by Citibank.[2]

If you're in a serious relationship, it's *absolutely critical* to communicate. If you don't, it'll cause a stress fracture that widens to a gap, then widens further to an irreconcilable abyss.

To move forward positively, you must first recognize that money invokes certain behaviors in you, and maybe in your partner, based on your family history and personal experiences. You may not have spent much time thinking about how much your childhood and/or certain family members influenced your habits. You may not have had the right opportunity to share your fears or concerns or challenges. Regarding money, you may not know the context or details of your partner's emotions and experiences.

Thus, the purpose of this workbook is to cement your relationship by sharing the details of your family, your history, your financial experience, your financial behavior, your habits, and your goals.

HOW TO USE THIS WORKBOOK

The recommended time and place to use this workbook is as follows: First, have a nice dinner at home. Second, open a special bottle of wine or a favorite beverage you can sip over the course of an hour or so, perched on the couch, with your sweetheart, this book, and a pen or pencil. The idea is to be relaxed and have an open discussion, sharing your history, where you are now, and thoughts of your future together.

It's inevitable that each of you has some regrets, and each of you has made some mistakes. But mistakes or missteps are a way to learn. We learn what not to do, we learn what we can do better, and we learn different strategies to approach our issues. And we learn to not put each other on a pedestal because we're both human.

> ### *But it's also inevitable that together there are more options, together more can be accomplished, and together you are a stronger unit than either of you are separately.*

I'd like to celebrate your strengths and wish you much happiness and joy as you embark on your life together!

So, clink your glasses together, and let's begin!

PART TWO

YOUR FINANCIAL EXPERIENCE

There must be a profound recognition that parents
are the first teachers and that education begins
before formal schooling and is deeply rooted in the values,
traditions, and norms of family and culture.

— Sara Lawrence-Lightfoot[3]

YOUR FAMILY HISTORY & BACKGROUND

Our family history and experiences growing up have a profound influence on our perceptions of money and the messages that play in our head about how money should be handled. Discovering and acknowledging these influences can be helpful, so that is why this set of questions is provided here.

1. **Was money discussed?**
   Bride: ❏ yes ❏ no
   Groom: ❏ yes ❏ no

2. **Who was in charge of paying bills?**
   Bride: ❏ Dad ❏ Mom ❏ Other
   Groom: ❏ Dad ❏ Mom ❏ Other

3. **Was there always "enough money"?**
   Bride: ❏ yes ❏ no
   Groom: ❏ yes ❏ no

4. **Were there money problems?**
   Bride: ❏ yes ❏ no
   Groom: ❏ yes ❏ no

FAMILY HISTORY – OBSERVATIONS

People learn different ways. Some by hearing, some by reading or watching. When it comes to money messages, our friends and families say certain things about their money beliefs and practices, and then we can observe what they do. Sometimes it matches what they say, sometimes not. We absorb their messages both ways. Let's dig in to find out what different money messages we've absorbed.

5. **What did you like about how family handled money?** (Check all that apply.)

LIKED	BRIDE	GROOM
Money saved by fixing things ourselves		
Money made from garage sales or bake sales		
Money made from collecting cans		
Money made from selling on Facebook Marketplace, Craigslist, or similar		
Dad's/Mom's pride at my first earned dollar from a part-time job		
Usually getting what I wanted from Mom/Dad		
Mom's pride in being able to afford things		
Painting or refinishing furniture to save money		
Birthday checks		
"Graduating" from McDonald's to Applebee's, then nicer restaurants as a family		

LIKED	BRIDE	GROOM
Getting new clothes		
Going on vacations to neat places		
Aunt & uncle's pride in being able to retire early		
Parents' savings/investments paid for part or all of my college		
Parents' pride in buying a new or bigger house		
Parents' pride on being able to help me with a down payment on a car or house		
Other		
Other		

6. **What didn't you like about how family handled money?**

DISLIKED	BRIDE	GROOM
Bill collectors calling		
Yelling/crying because of bill collectors		
Parents fighting over money issues		
Lying over lost money		

DISLIKED	BRIDE	GROOM
Money lost to gambling		
Money lost to other bad habits		
Clipping coupons		
Missing events because we couldn't afford to attend		
Shabby clothes		
Shopping for used clothing		
Missed meals because money was short		
Having to earn my own spending money		
Parent having to take a second job to pay the bills		
Money crises because there was no emergency fund		
Parents' need to "keep up" with the Joneses (with new cars, etc.)		
Other		
Other		

7. **Did you receive an allowance or hold a part-time job when growing up?**

Bride: ❑ yes ❑ no

Groom: ❑ yes ❑ no

8. **How did you spend your earnings?**

HOW MONEY IS SPENT	BRIDE	GROOM
Eating out		
Candy		
Buying music		
Buying clothes		
Going to the movies or a show		
Paying for a date		
Gas or repairs for the car		
Car payment		
Savings		
Other		

9. What expectations were given to you about money?

Sometimes expectations are specifically stated by family or friends. Sometimes they are implied. Sometimes unexpected or uncommon expenses come up or are situational. Let's examine this further.

"YOU SHOULD..."	BRIDE	GROOM
Pay for your own clothes		
Pay for your car expenses		
Be responsible for your own entertainment		
Pay your own way through college		
Help others (family) when you can		
Help others less fortunate (charity/tithe)		
Save for a rainy day		
NOT trust banks		
Use money to show your success		
Not flaunt your money		

ROLE MODELS

10. **Who are your role models?** (Check all that apply.)

ROLE MODEL	BRIDE	GROOM
Mom		
Dad		
Grandma		
Grandpa		
Aunt or uncle		
Cousin		
Other relative		

11. **Why are they your role models?**

How do you define financial success, and who's your financial role model?

REASON	ROLE MODEL	BRIDE	GROOM
Always had enough to eat			
Always had a place to live/never evicted			
Always had a job and earnings			
They had a lot of possessions—house, car, jewelry, clothes, etc.—that I admired			
Had health insurance, so not ruined by medical costs			
Started a company that's doing well			
Minimal debt; no payday loans or bill collectors hounding them			
Enough savings so an emergency didn't ruin them			
Generous to me			
Other			

ROLE MODELS OUTSIDE YOUR FAMILY

The big secret in life is there is no big secret. Whatever your goal..., you can get there—as long as you're willing to be honest with yourself about the preparation and work involved.

— Attributed to many sources, including Oprah, Wayne Dyer, the movie The Secret, and others.[4]

12. **Who are your money role models outside of family?** (Check all that apply.)

WHO	BRIDE	GROOM
Friend's parent		
Prominent businessperson in town		
Beyonce, Madame CJ Walker, Taylor Swift, Martha Stewart, Oprah, or other celebrity		
Elon Musk, Mark Zuckerberg, Steven Jobs, Bill Gates, Tyler Perry, or other business billionaire		
Famous pro athlete		
Celebrity		
Other		

13. Why are they your role models?

REASON	BRIDE	GROOM
They are rich—have big house, fancy cars, jewelry, vacation homes, etc.		
They accumulated a lot of financial assets such as stocks, bonds, funds.		
They started a business that's known to be doing well.		
There is a scholarship or program named after them or initiated by them.		
They give to the community they live in.		
They are known philanthropists & made a big donation in a recent crisis.		
They are generous to family and friends.		
They were able to retire early.		

EXPERIENCES

YOUR MONEY HABITS

14. **Were you aware of the investing experiences your family had?**

   Bride: ☐ yes   ☐ no

   Groom: ☐ yes   ☐ no

15. **Who was in charge of investing and saving?**

   Bride: ☐ Dad   ☐ Mom   ☐ Both

   Groom: ☐ Dad   ☐ Mom   ☐ Both

16. **Were they good investors?**

   Bride: ☐ yes   ☐ no   ☐ don't know

   Groom: ☐ yes   ☐ no   ☐ don't know

17. **Have you ever lent money to a family member or friend?**

   Bride: ☐ yes   ☐ no

   Groom: ☐ yes   ☐ no

18. **What happened?**

EXPERIENCE	BRIDE	GROOM
Fully paid back		
Partially paid back		
Never paid back		
Person avoided me		
Person thought it was a gift		
Someone else paid it back		
Included in a bankruptcy & never paid back		

LENDING & BORROWING QUESTIONS

While sometimes there are social pressures to lend, or pressures to borrow to buy something compelling or to take a trip, doing so puts your capital at risk (lending) or can increase the amount of debt and interest you're paying (borrowing). So, it's practical to evaluate what you've done in the past and to be aware of the current obligations. Also—maybe—it's time to set some guide rails on this for your new joint life.

19. **Are you likely to lend money again?**

    Bride: ❑ yes   ❑ no

    Groom: ❑ yes   ❑ no

20. **How likely are you to borrow money from a family member or friend?**

    Bride: ❑ very likely   ❑ somewhat likely   ❑ unlikely

    Groom: ❑ very likely   ❑ somewhat likely   ❑ unlikely

21. **Have you borrowed money before?**

        Bride: ❏ yes ❏ no

        Groom: ❏ yes ❏ no

22. **How often?**

FREQUENCY	BRIDE	GROOM
Never		
Once in your life		
Once or twice a year		
Several times a year		
Monthly		
Weekly		
Other		

23. **Are you likely to borrow again?**

        Bride: ❏ yes ❏ no

        Groom: ❏ yes ❏ no

BORROWING DISCUSSION

24. **Under what circumstances would you borrow money from family or friends?**

SITUATION	BRIDE	GROOM
Crisis		
Car accident/failure/major repairs		
Car payment due		
Refrigerator out of order with $100s in groceries at risk of spoiling		
Medical expenses		
Power outage		
Large utility bills/risk of utility shut-off		
Risk of utility turnoff		
Risk of eviction		
Help a relative or good friend		
Shopping because you're depressed		
Other		

HABITS

The reason most people never reach their goals is they don't define them or ever seriously consider them believable or achievable. Winners can tell you where they are going, what they plan to do along the way, and who will be sharing the adventure with them.

—Denis Waitley

25. **Do you currently spend what you earn, more than you earn, or less than you earn?**

        Bride: ☐ spend exactly ☐ spend more ☐ spend less

        Groom: ☐ spend exactly ☐ spend more ☐ spend less

26. **What level of balance in your checking account is a comfortable level?**

        Bride: $_____   Groom: $_____

27. **What level balance in your savings or money market account is a comfortable level?**

        Bride: $_____   Groom: $_____

28. **Do you like saving and investing?**

Bride: ☐ yes ☐ no

Groom: ☐ yes ☐ no

INVESTING QUESTIONS

Having an emergency fund and investing are great ways to build for the future. Doing so can enable you to go on vacations, create the home you want, and provide for a growing, merged, or extended family. Investing is a great financial practice to help you build the joint life and lifestyle you want.

29. **What kind of investments have you made?**

TYPE	BRIDE	GROOM
Stocks		
Bonds		
Certificates of deposit		
Mutual funds		
Variable annuities		
Partnerships		
Real estate: apartment building, duplex, time share, etc.		
Precious metals		
Collectibles		

TYPE	BRIDE	GROOM
Friend/family member's business		
Own business		
Other		

30. **a) Have your experiences been good or bad?**

       Bride: ❏ good ❏ bad

       Groom: ❏ good ❏ bad

   b) What made it good or bad?

Bride: _____

Groom: _____

FAMILY MONEY HISTORY CONTEXT

Past family money crises often have profound effects on an individual's beliefs and feelings about money. Usually, your parents or grandparents will talk about them, or maybe you heard them fighting or conversations with raised voices on these topics. It's important to identify and be aware of these, as usually they lead to strong feelings on certain money topics.

31. Which of the following money-related crises are part of your family's history or that of close friends? (Check all that apply.)

CRISIS	BRIDE	GROOM
Family member lived through the Depression.		
Family member died without life insurance.		
Someone I knew lost a business.		
Someone I knew had a family member in a mental institution he/she was supporting.		
Company of someone I know failed and took the pension with it, so he had to keep working at age 70.		
Friend's parent retired in early 2000s, but after the huge stock market drop in 2008, had to go back to work at age 66.		
Young relative declined health insurance at work then had thousands in medical expenses.		
Friend or relative had sick baby or child.		

CRISIS	BRIDE	GROOM
Someone I knew had multiple vet surgeries for a dear pet.		
Professional I knew was laid off and out of work for more than a year.		
Someone I knew lost everything due to divorce or sudden widowhood.		
Someone I knew had a gambling or drug problem.		
Other		

YOUR MONEY HISTORY

People's understanding of bankruptcy doesn't always reflect reality. A bankruptcy will follow you around 7 years or longer on your credit report—continuing to limit your credit. It's really an awful financial decision and should be avoided! However, in the spirit of openness and full disclosure, this is the time to fess up if it happened…and the time to put good financial habits in place so it never happens again!

32. **Have you ever had a bankruptcy or been close?**

Bride: ❑ yes   ❑ no

Groom: ❑ yes   ❑ no

33. **If yes, how long ago?**

Bride: _____ years

Groom: _____ years

34. What happened? (Check all that apply.)

SITUATION	BRIDE	GROOM
Medical bills		
Business failed		
Credit cards out of control		
Divorce		
Family member in trouble		
Disabled family member		
Family member on drugs		
Caring for aging family member		
Out-of-control payday or title loan(s)		
Bad real estate investment		
Gambling		
Loan to family member or friend not paid back		
Other		

PART THREE

WHERE ARE YOU NOW?

You are in control of your life. Don't ever forget that.
You are what you are because of the conscious
and subconscious choices you have made.

— Barbara Hall[5]

35. **What is your current income—from salary, side jobs, commissions, and bonuses combined?**

BRIDE		
Salary main job, commissions, bonuses	Side jobs, gig jobs, cash jobs	Total

GROOM		
Salary main job, commissions, bonuses	Side jobs, gig jobs, cash jobs	Total

SPENDING & EXPENSES

A lot of people pay bills without thinking about them. A great way to start financial planning is to have a written budget and to think about what you're spending and why. An annual budget self-checkup can sometimes "find" money that can be applied to higher priorities. Budgeting is a way to make sure your spending matches your values. See Part Five for more budgeting tools.

36. Are you a spender or saver?

Bride: ❑ Spender ❑ Saver ❑ Mix of both

Groom: ❑ Spender ❑ Saver ❑ Mix of both

37. Do you have student loans?

Bride: ❑ yes ❑ no

Groom: ❑ yes ❑ no

Student loans are necessary for most students to get the college education and credentials needed for good-paying jobs. They are also an obligation to take seriously. They affect your credit report. They don't "go away" in bankruptcy.

38. How much do you owe in student loans? List each loan, monthly payment, and its terms.

BRIDE			
Loan Name	Term (years)	Monthly Payment ($)	Remaining Balance ($)
GSL			
University loan			
Bank loan			
Other			

GROOM			
Loan Name	Term (years)	Monthly Payment ($)	Remaining Balance ($)
GSL			
University loan			
Bank loan			
Other			

WHERE ARE YOU NOW—CREDIT CARDS?

A credit card is a monthly loan you're getting from the bank. It's not your money; it's theirs. And for the privilege of a revolving line of credit, you (usually) pay high interest.

39. Assuming you have credit cards, how did you feel when you got your first credit card?

FEELING	BRIDE	GROOM
Like it was play money (not mine)		
Ready to go shopping!		
Excited		
Afraid of the responsibility		
Other		

40. What's your philosophy on credit cards?

PHILOSOPHY	BRIDE	GROOM
I deserve to enjoy myself.		
It'll supplement my low salary until I get a raise or that new job.		
Now I can buy decent presents.		
It's only for emergencies.		
It's only for car repair.		
It'll help me establish credit.		
As long as I keep up with the minimum payments, I'll be fine.		
Other		

41. When do you use credit cards and why?

USE CREDIT CARDS FOR...	BRIDE	GROOM
Eating out		
Entertainment with friends		
Only for emergencies		

USE CREDIT CARDS FOR...	BRIDE	GROOM
Only for car repair		
Presents		
All spending since I get money back or miles or merchandise		
Groceries		
Travel		
Business expenses		
Treating myself after a bad day		
Other		

42. How much do you pay on your credit card each month?

Bride: ❑ Whole balance
❑ More than minimum, but always carry over a balance
❑ Pay minimum

Groom: ❑ Whole balance
❑ More than minimum, but always carry over a balance
❑ Pay minimum

MORE ON CREDIT CARDS

43. List your credit cards. How much is the balance on each? What's your minimum payment? How much do you pay on each? What's the interest rate? How much interest did you pay last year?

BRIDE					
Card Name/ Type	Balance	Minimum Payment	Your Monthly Payment	Interest Rate	Total Interest Paid Last Year

GROOM					
Card Name/ Type	Balance	Minimum Payment	Your Monthly Payment	Interest Rate	Total Interest Paid Last Year

WHERE ARE YOU NOW—CAR DEBT?

44. How much do you owe on your cars?

CAR MODEL/ YEAR	LOAN BALANCE	TIME LEFT (YR/MO)	MONTHLY PAYMENT	BRIDE OR GROOM?

45. Do you prefer to buy or lease a car?

Bride: ❑ Buy ❑ Lease

Groom: ❑ Buy ❑ Lease

46. Do you prefer a new or used car?

Bride: ❑ New ❑ Used

Groom: ❑ New ❑ Used

47. **What's your philosophy on car ownership?**

PHILOSOPHY	BRIDE	GROOM
Keep until the car dies		
Keep for 10 years		
Keep for 100,000 miles		
Get a new one when the loan is paid off		
Car must be nice—part of my image		
Replace when big expenses start		
Just need basic transportation		
Other		

WHERE ARE YOU NOW—HOUSING BASICS?

48. **How long have you been living independently?**

    Bride: _____ years

    Groom: _____ years

49. **Do you own or rent?**

    Bride: ☐ Own ☐ Rent

    Groom: ☐ Own ☐ Rent

50. **If you rent, how much do you pay monthly?**

    Bride: $_____ Groom: $_____

51. **If you own, how much do you pay monthly for mortgage, insurance, property tax?**

    Bride: $_____ Groom: $_____

52. **If you own your home, in what year did you buy?**

    Bride: _____ Groom: _____

53. **If you own your home, how much were you able to put down?**

    Bride: $_____ or _____%

    Groom: $_____ or _____%

54. **How long is your loan? What interest rate?**

    Bride: _____years at _____%

    Groom: _____years at _____%

55. **Have you refinanced lately?**

    Bride: ☐ yes ☐ no   date_____

    Groom: ☐ yes ☐ no   date_____

56. Reason for refinancing?

REASON	BRIDE	GROOM
Better interest rate		
Consolidate/pay off credit cards		
Pay off or consolidate other debt, payday or title loans		
Pay off medical bills		
Finish basement, fix up bathroom, etc.		
Pay college tuition for son, daughter, or other relative		
Job loss		
Eliminate lingering school loans		
Cash for new business		
Divorced/widowed		
Other		

57. **Have you refinanced previously?**

Bride: ☐ yes ☐ no year_____

Groom: ☐ yes ☐ no year_____

58. **What rate and terms did you get with the refinance?**

	RATE	TERMS
Bride		
Groom		

EVERYDAY EXPENSES

As those persons who despair of ever being rich make little account
of small expenses, thinking that little added to
a little will never make any great sum.

—Plutarch[6]

59. **How much do you spend each month eating out and for entertainment?**

Bride: $_____ Eating out $_____ Entertainment

Groom: $_____ Eating out $_____ Entertainment

60. **How much do you spend on clothing each month?**

Bride: $_____   Groom $_____

61. **How much do you spend on gifts each month?**

Bride: $_____   Groom $_____

62. **How much do you spend on phone, internet, movies, & streaming each month?**

Bride: $_____   Groom $_____

63. **Any hobbies or collectibles? What are they? How much do you spend a month?**

Bride: Hobby name: _____ $_____

Groom: Hobby name: _____ $_____

EXPENSES RELATED TO HEALTH & FAMILY

Health insurance is one of the smartest expenses to always include in your monthly budget. Checkups are key to catching serious health conditions early when they are more likely curable. More importantly, hospital expenses from an accident or serious illness (like COVID) can easily run into thousands of dollars and ruin the best-laid financial plans. Health insurance is one of the best ways to protect your finances!

64. **Do you have health, dental, and vision insurance through work? How much do you pay per month?**

Bride: $_____ Groom: $_____

65. **Do you have health and/or dental and vision insurance on your own? How much do you pay per month?**

Bride: $_____ Groom: $_____

LIFE INSURANCE

If you are married, have a child, and/or have substantial debt, life insurance will be something to consider. It's cheaper when you're young and healthy. It can be budget friendly. Note: It's not necessary for everyone.

66. Do you have life insurance—either through group coverage at work or other personally owned coverage?

Bride: ❑ yes ❑ no

Groom: ❑ yes ❑ no

67. Is your life insurance type "permanent "or "term," and what's the face amount of coverage?

PERM OR TERM	FACE AMOUNT	TERM (YEARS)	BRIDE	GROOM
Example: Term	$500,000	20 years	X	

RETIREMENT PLANNING

"Pay yourself first" is a common refrain in financial planning. The first way is health insurance. Second is an emergency fund. Third is participating in a retirement plan. Participate as early as possible. Time is on your side. The time value of money means early contributions have much longer to grow. Ultimately, you will have to sock away less if you start earlier.

BENEFITS OFFERED THROUGH WORK PAYROLL DEDUCTION

68. Does your work offer a 401(k) or other types of group retirement plans? What type of plan? (Check all that apply.)

PLAN TYPE	BRIDE	GROOM
401(k)		
403(b)		
Simple IRA		
Profit Sharing		

PLAN TYPE	BRIDE	GROOM
ESOP		
Defined Benefit Plan		
Deferred Comp		
Other		

69. Do you participate? How much do you contribute per month in dollars or percentage of income?

	PARTICIPATE (YES/NO)	$ AMOUNT OR %
Bride		
Groom		

70. Do you take advantage of the employer match? (That's free money!)

Bride: ❏ yes   ❏ no

Groom: ❏ yes   ❏ no

WEDDING FINANCES

71. **Do you have a wedding savings account? What's the balance?**

☐ yes   ☐ no   Balance: $_____

72. **Do you have a wedding budget?**

Bride: ☐ yes   ☐ no

Groom: ☐ yes   ☐ no

Together: $_____

73. **How much are parents/relatives paying, and how much are you paying?**

BRIDE'S FAMILY	GROOM'S FAMILY	BRIDE	GROOM

74. **Now that you know what things cost, have you discussed trade-offs to make sure important items are included without "breaking the bank"?**

: ❑ yes ❑ no

75. **Are you comfortable with how much you are spending for the wedding and honeymoon?**

Bride: ❑ yes ❑ no

Groom: ❑ yes ❑ no

PART FOUR

STEPS FOR CREATING FINANCIAL COMPATIBILITY

A goal without a plan is just a wish.

—Attributed to Antoine de Saint-Exupéry[7]

DEFINING HAPPILY EVER AFTER (Financially)

76. What does your happily ever after look like? How would you define "happy ever after" in terms of your money communication and experience as a couple?

BRIDE	GROOM

77. **How do you plan to handle banking/checking accounts after you're married?**
    ❑ Keep separate accounts

    ❑ Have all income and expenses flow from a joint account

    ❑ A combination of separate accounts for some things and joint account for household expenses?

78. **Have you discussed how to divide the household bills?**
    Bride: ❑ yes ❑ no
    Groom: ❑ yes ❑ no

79. **Will you weight or pro-rate contributions to monthly bills based on respective income?**
    Bride: ❑ yes ❑ no
    Groom: ❑ yes ❑ no

80. **Will you divide bills by some other formula?**

    Describe :_____

81. **Have you discussed how finances will change when you have children?**
    Bride: ❑ yes ❑ no
    Groom: ❑ yes ❑ no

82. **Will one parent stay home or both continue working in some capacity?**
    ❑ One stay at home

    ❑ Both continue working

83. **What's your philosophy on how to fund college for your kids?**
Many people have strong feelings on who contributes what and whether the kid should have "skin" in the game.
    ❑ We pay both tuition and board/books

    ❑ We pay part and they pay part

    ❑ They should fund the whole thing through work and loans

ACCOUNTABILITY

84. **At what dollar amount of purchase or sale should a spouse confer with you? For what type of purchase?**

AMOUNT	TYPE OF PURCHASE	BRIDE	GROOM
Ex: $200	Clothing, jewelry		
	Vehicles		
	Electronic devices		
	Children's sports/ equipment		

AMOUNT	TYPE OF PURCHASE	BRIDE	GROOM
	Birthday or holiday gifts		
	Vacations		
	Other		

85. At what amount of debt or obligation should a spouse confer with you? For what types of debts or loans? Ask spouse to approve the debt first; if yes, above what limit should your spouse discuss it with you?

AMOUNT	TYPE OF DEBT	BRIDE	GROOM
Ex: $400	Clothing, jewelry		
	Car purchase or lease		
	Apartment rental/home mortgage		

AMOUNT	TYPE OF DEBT	BRIDE	GROOM
	Large department store/credit card purchase		
	Rental furniture contract		
	Payday or title loan		
	Loan from family member or friend		
	Cash advance		
	Large gift purchases		
	Vacation or event tickets		
	Other		

WRITTEN COMMITMENTS

1. I, _____, and _____

   promise to pay off credit cards by _____ (date).

2. I, _____, promise to limit my spending on

   _____ to $_____/month.

3. I, _____, promise to limit my spending on

   _____ to $_____/month.

4. We both promise to confer with each other before making any large purchases for

   amounts more than $_____.

5. I/we, _____,

   promise to start/increase savings by $_____ per month.

6. We both promise to inform each other if any of the following events occur:
   - ❏ Car accident
   - ❏ Traffic ticket
   - ❏ Unexpected liability/debt
   - ❏ New liability/debt threat
   - ❏ Job change or job loss

7. We both promise to confer with each other before making large money decisions, taking on a new regular household expense or contractual obligation, refinancing student loans or house or car, quitting or changing jobs, or making a decision about moving (especially to another city or state). Initial here to indicate your agreement.

   Bride: _____   Groom: _____

8. We both promise to select a financial mentor (family or friend) or, if unavailable, a financial advisor—after our wedding—to help guide us through important financial decisions and dilemmas over time. Initial here to indicate agreement.

Bride: _____   Groom: _____

9. We both promise (add commitment #9 here): _____

_____

_____.

10. We both promise (add commitment #10 here): _____

_____

_____.

Committed to by:

Bride: _____.

Groom: _____.

Today's date: _____

PART FIVE

TOOLS

Experience is not what happens to you;
it's what you do with what happens to you.

—Aldous Huxley

If you would be wealthy, think of saving as well as getting.

—Ben Franklin

OUR WEDDING BUDGET

Use this worksheet to create a plan with your future partner. This will help you both stay accountable and on track.

	ESTIMATE	ACTUAL
BEAUTY Hair & Makeup Manicure & Pedicure Gratuity		$150-800/person
CAKE | DESSERT		$600-1,500
CELEBRANT Gratuity		$300-800
MUSIC DJ Live Band Ceremony Musicians/Soloists		$800-2,500
DRESS Wedding Gown Alterations & Pressing Accessories		$1,000-5,000
FAVORS Parent Gifts Wedding Party Gifts Guest Favors		$200-1,000
FLOWERS | DECOR Bouquets Boutonnieres Ceremony Flowers Receptions Flowers		$2,000-8,000
HOTEL		$300-1,000
OTHER ENTERTAINMENT Photobooth, Caricature Artist		$1,000-4,000

	ESTIMATE	ACTUAL
PHOTOGRAPHER		
Photography (6-8 hours)		
Gratuity		
Album		$2,500–6,000
RECEPTION VENUE		
Venue Rental		
Food & Beverages		
Gratuity		$10,000–30,000
REHEARSAL DINNER		$25-100/person
RINGS		
Wedding Band #1		
Wedding Band #2		$300–1,500/person
STATIONERY		
Save the Date		
Invitation Suite		
Reception Paper Goods		
Guest Book		$500–1,500
TRANSPORTATION		$800–2,000
TUXEDO | SUITS | ACCESSORIES		$200-500/person
VIDEOGRAPHER		
Video (4-6 hours)		
Gratuity		$2,000–7,000
WEDDING PLANNER | COORDINATOR		$2,500-10,000
MISCELLANEOUS		
Reserve for the unexpected		$500

OTHER WEDDING RESOURCES

WEBSITES FOR WEDDING PLANNING:
- The Knot (www.theknot.com)
- Wedding Wire (www.weddingwire.com)
- Zola (www.zola.com)
- Brides (www.brides.com)
- Martha Stewart Weddings (www.marthastewart.com/6417/weddings)
- Wedding Bee (www.weddingbee.com)
- MyWedding (www.mywedding.com)
- Style Me Pretty (www.stylemepretty.com)
- Junebug Weddings (junebugweddings.com)
- Wedding Lovely (weddinglovely.com)

RESOURCES FOR HONEYMOON PLANNING:

- Tripadvisor (www.tripadvisor.com)
- Expedia (www.expedia.com)
- KAYAK (www.kayak.com)
- Honeymoons (honeymoons.com)
- Travelocity (www.travelocity.com)
- Honeyfund (www.honeyfund.com)
- Travelzoo (www.travelzoo.com)
- Jetsetter (www.jetsetter.com)
- Honeymoon Wishes (www.honeymoonwishes.com)
- Destify Destination Weddings (destify.com)

AFTER-WEDDING BUDGETING BASICS

WHAT IS A BUDGET?

- Budget = INCOME – EXPENSES
- Income includes salary, wages, commissions, payments and cash from every source; side gigs, family gifts, government assistance etc.
- Expenses include bills, debt payments, cash out for every purpose: rent, utilities, food, etc.
- Cookie jar method:

This is when you take every receipt for a month and put it in a cookie jar or shoe box. Make up slips of paper for coffee, etc., without a receipt. Then add up each category and put in the following budget worksheet.

Be aware: There are two categories of spending.

- WANTS

and

- NEEDS

POST-WEDDING BUDGET WORKSHEET

INCOME	MONTHLY	ANNUAL
Salary or wages – person 1		
Salary or wages – person 2		
Gig work, side job, or second job income		
Alimony or child support		
Government Assistance /SNAP/Disability Income/Social Security		
TOTAL INCOME		

FIXED EXPENSES	MONTHLY	ANNUAL
Housing – rent or mortgage		
Phone		
Car payment & car insurance		
Debt payments – loans		
Debt payments – credit cards		
Tech basics (internet, streaming)		

FIXED EXPENSES	MONTHLY	ANNUAL
Other fixed expenses		
SUBTOTAL FIXED EXPENSES		

VARIABLE EXPENSES	MONTHLY	ANNUAL
Groceries		
Transportation (gas, Uber, bus, metro)		
Medical/dental out-of-pocket costs		
Day care or babysitting		
Utilities (gas, electric, sewer, water, cable, etc.)		
College funding/contributions		
Household supplies (cleaning supplies, paper towels, personal hygiene, etc.)		
Retirement contributions (401(k), Simple IRA, 403(b), IRA)		
SUBTOTAL VARAIABLE EXPENSES		

DISCRETIONARY EXPENSES	MONTHLY	ANNUAL
Restaurants		
Gifts: holiday, birthday, special occasion		
Travel & vacations		
Entertainment/hobbies		
Vacations/travel		
Charity/tithing		
Savings/emergency funds		
Vet & other pet costs		
SUBTOTAL DISCRETIONARY EXPENSES		
TOTAL EXPENSES		
TOTAL INCOME – TOTAL EXPENSE		
SURPLUS OR	DEFICIT	

FINANCIAL
DECISION TREE

YOU, THE CLIENT

INCOME PROTECTION
- CASH MANAGEMENT
- ASSET PROTECTION
- DISABILITY

RETIREMENT
- INVESTMENT
- CORPORATE PLAN
- SOCIAL SECURITY
- HEALTH CARE

ASSIST CHILDREN
- PREP/ COLLEGE
- LIVING EXPENSES

ASSIST PARENTS
- RETIREMENT
- LONG TERM CARE
- FINAL COSTS

ESTATE PLAN
- WILLS/ PLANNING
- TRUST STRATEGIES
- LEGACY FOR HEIRS
- CHARITABLE GIVING

As seen in:

St. Charles County
Business Record
St. Charles County's Daily Business and Legal Newspaper

Friday, January 31, 2003
Vol. 52, No. 22

DOLAN MEDIA COMPANY

Women in Business

Concepts to help you control your financial destiny

By Nina N. Swartz, MBA

Here's an introduction to key concepts worth studying further on your own or discussing at length with a trusted financial advisor.

▶ **Cash Management**

The first tenet of cash management is saving. To get ahead financially, spend less than you earn and save at least 10% of every paycheck. The second is -have an **emergency fund.** This is a separate savings or money market account that ideally should be equal to 3-6 months of expenses. This account should be held in reserve and accessed rarely - only in case of extreme need - such as major unexpected car repairs, to cover expenses during temporary unemployment, etc.

▶ **Compounding**

When you put money in an interest bearing account, a Certificate of Deposit, or a bond, you earn interest. Conversely, many stocks pay dividends. Initially, you earn interest or dividends on the original principal invested. Next you have to decide what to do with that dividend or interest. If you reinvest in more shares or cross-invest into another investment, you earn interest on the interest. Compounding is the return earned on both the principal and the accumulated interest from prior periods.

▶ **Time Value of Money**

The time value of money is the idea that a dollar now is worth more than dollar in the future, even after adjusting for inflation, because a dollar now can earn interest or other appreciation until the time the dollar in the future would be received.

▶ **Asset Classes**

There are three major categories of assets: stocks, bonds and cash. **Stock** represents partial ownership in a public company. Companies sell ownership in themselves to raise money to grow. In exchange for money, you get a portion of shares of ownership, sometimes a dividend or portion of their earnings, and usually a voice or vote in how they run the company.

Corporations and governments also raise capital through the sale of bonds. A **bond** is a promise of the issuer (borrower) to pay a specified amount of principal and interest to

the bondholder (lender) at specified times in the future. In other words, a bond is like a loan. An investor buys a bond (lends his/her money) and the corporation or government agrees to buy the bond back on a designated date (the maturity date) and to pay interest at regular intervals between the purchase date and maturity date. There are several types of bonds - corporate bonds, which are loans to companies; government bonds which are loans to the US government; and municipal bonds, which are loans to city, state or local governments.

Cash as a category is used to represent very liquid accounts such as money market accounts, NOW accounts, checking accounts, or actual cash. Cash represents readily available funds.

▶ **Asset Allocation**

While it's useful to divide your investable dollars into different asset classes, it is also advantageous to further **diversify** or divide your investments in each asset class. Stocks and equity funds can first be differentiated by growth or value characteristics, and then by size. Some stocks are called **growth stocks** because the companies are relatively young and are in a growth spurt of business, where cash is tight, but sales and income are growing. **Value stocks** are stocks of companies that are more established, where sales and income is flat but steady. Next, stocks can be broken down by the size of the company. There are large company or large capitalization stocks (called **large cap** for short), middle sized companies or **mid cap**, and small sized companies or **small cap**. International or global stocks or funds can fall into any of these categories.

Likewise, bond or fixed income investments can be further differentiated by type of bond and length of maturity. (Note: While there is no guarantee that a diversified portfolio will outperform a non-diversified portfolio, or that diversification among different asset classes will reduce risk, by diversifying, you can improve the probability of positive returns.)

▶ **Dollar Cost Averaging (DCA)**

DCA is an investing technique in which you invest the same amount of money in stocks or mutual funds each month, quarter,

or year. Since share prices vary, your dollars buy a different number of shares each interval. The advantages of this strategy are that it requires no effort to "time" the market (such efforts usually fail), and it automatically causes you to buy more shares when they are cheap and fewer when they are expensive. This is a popular way to invest since it allows you to "pay yourself first" by automatically sending money from your checking account to your IRA or mutual fund account every month.

▶ **Inflation, Real Returns**

When the costs of bread or stamps go up, it takes you more dollars to buy the same goods. **Inflation** is the measure of how much costs of goods and services have increased in a given period of time. **Real return** is a measure of how much you really retain from a given investment after adjusted by inflation and taxes. For example, if a stock has a 6% total return, reduce that by -2.3% inflation and by taxes (28% of 6% is about 2%), therefore 6% - 2.3% - 2% = 1.7% real return.

▶ **Rebalancing**

While being well diversified among asset classes and their sub-categories is ideal, just being diversified is not where your planning process ends. Conduct regular "check-ups" to see if your investments are accomplishing what was intended. **Rebalancing** is making adjustments to counteract the fact that different assets have performed differently and now comprise different percentages of the assets than intended.

In summary, it's essential to educate yourself about financial choices and to be proactive. If you commit to being as good a consumer of your finances as you are when you buy a house, car, vacation etc., *you should be able to control your financial success. **Remember, it's not how much you make, but how much you save and invest that determines wealth.** To find out more about investing resources and web-sites,* send an email to: nswartz@pfpadvisor.com

Reprinted by permission   *DOLAN MEDIA COMPANY*   Friday, March 12, 2003 • Vol. 133, No. 51

The Countian

St. Louis County Edition

Daily Business and Legal News Since 1902

How much life insurance do I need?

Nina N. Swartz
Premier Financial Partners

Most of us don't make enough or save enough to self-insure. That is to say, whether we rely on two incomes or just one income to pay our bills and support our family, we don't have enough savings or investments to cover all our family's needs without that person's salary and benefits. So the purpose of life insurance is to replace the income that person would have earned over his or her lifetime that would have been used for family needs.

So how much life insurance do you need? While many insurance agents will tell you that you need 5 times your annual income or 10 times your annual income, an ethical financial advisor or agent will instead ask you:

"What do you want life insurance to accomplish for you?"

The big expected expenses are usually considered first:
• Do you want it to pay off the house?
• Do you want it to cover the costs of college for your children?
• Do you want it to pay off all your family debts and liabilities, including car loans, credit cards, student loans, etc.?

The next areas of consideration are unique one-time expenses:
• Do you want it to cover final costs (funeral, service, etc.)?
• Do you want it to cover probate or executor costs?
• Do you want it to cover costs relating to selling your house (if you're single) or of distributing assets to relatives out of town?

The next areas of consideration are the daily needs of your beneficiaries or survivors:
• Do you want it to cover your portion of the household bills, expenses, etc. so your beneficiaries can maintain the lifestyle they currently enjoy?
• Do you want to provide for transportation if one of your loved ones has an unreliable or dangerous vehicle or doesn't have their own car at all?
• Do you want to provide an emergency fund?
• Do you want it to provide retirement income, so your beneficiaries don't have to work in old age?

While the 10 areas of consideration listed above represent the most common priorities of individuals when evaluating insurance needs, each of these areas requires further clarification. For example, when planning for college, did you want to provide your children with a full ride, i.e. tuition, room, board, books, etc.? Did you want to provide a portion of this? Did you want to plan on providing enough for a private university (for example: Washington University at $40,000 per year for a full ride) or a public college (such as Mizzou at $11,500 per year for a full ride). Did you want to provide for graduate school, if they are interested? Did you want to provide for transportation to get to school and or a vehicle at school?

When considering how much to supplement income of a loved one, do you want to provide enough so he or she doesn't have to work at all, work part time, or do you assume they will have to work full time and have some kind of supplemental support? If some kind of support seems reasonable, how many years should that support be provided?

Additionally, insurance can be "structured" to provide different levels of coverage at different times of life. For example, you may want the highest coverage up to and including children's college years. After college is complete, you may not need that $200,000 portion of coverage, so why pay for it? Conversely, what if you or someone in the family develops diabetes or cancer and either cannot get insurance or can only get coverage if they pay several times more than someone with average health. With certain types of insurance products, you can upgrade from temporary coverage to permanent coverage to address that need.

These are complicated, multifaceted decisions. That is why it makes sense to consult with a caring, local financial advisor or insurance professional to both educate you and to help you think through all the micro decisions that go into the big bottom line decision of how much do you need.

Securities and Investment Advisory services offered through WS Griffith Securities, Inc. Member NASD/SIPC. 12655 Olive Blvd., Suite 495, St. Louis, MO 63141. (314)-576-1166. Premier Financial Partners is separate from WS Griffith Securities, Inc. and is not a broker/dealer.

Author and Financial Advisor Nina Swartz has 20 years of financial services experience and conducts her value oriented practice in Creve Coeur MO from the offices of Premier Financial Partners. She can be reached for a no-obligation meeting by calling 314-576-1166x222 or emailing nswartz@premierfn.com

ST. LOUIS Small Business Monthly

SBM

The Source for Business Owners

VOL. 17, ISSUE I

FEBRUARY 2004

How To Grade Your Financial Adviser

by Nina Swartz

For those of you who have thought about your situation for quite some time and finally selected a financial adviser, financial planner or stockbroker, I have a question: Now that you're part of the "in crowd," how do you know if your adviser is doing a good job for you? Have you ever graded him or her?

Credentials/Titles

Titles and job descriptions vary by firm and can have a variety of meanings. For example, some "discount" brokers give advice; some do not. Some "discount" brokers offer discounts on stock trades but charge full mark-ups or commissions on other investment choices. Some "full-service" firms offer more choices than others.

To avoid an entire article on this topic, let me summarize by saying some titles represent actual designations and rigorous testing, whereas others are marketing spins on functional titles.

For example, if the name on the door is that of a life insurance firm, the salespeople will have a life and health insurance license and possibly a Series 6 Securities license. The life and health license enables the individual to present and sell term insurance, universal life and whole life. The Series 6 license enables the individual to present and sell variable equity and insurance products.

Conversely, anyone calling him/herself a stockbroker has to pass the more rigorous Series 7 General Securities exam that qualifies the individual to sell any publicly traded investment, including: stocks, corporate/government/municipal bonds, options, mutual funds, other variable equity products and certain nonpublicly traded investments such as limited partnerships. A Series 7 exam includes a great deal on exchange and market rules, products, regulations, ethics and suitability. Continuing education is required to keep both

life insurance and variable product licenses current and valid.

A number of higher-level credentials exist, such as the Certified Financial Planner (CFP) and the Chartered Financial Consultant (ChFC). The CFP program, first introduced in 1972, includes five unit exams and a sixth, intense, two-day final exam. The applicant must have at least two years of experience to apply. Given the 100-plus hours of study required for each exam, the entire CFP course is usually tackled over a several-year period. The comprehensive material covers insurance, investments, retirement planning, tax planning and estate planning.

The ChFC exam was introduced in 1982 as a financial-planning designation for insurance professionals. The applicant must have at least three years of experience and must pass 10 unit exams. The ChFC course covers the same topics in a similarly comprehensive approach and during a similarly lengthy study and test period. Both the CFP and ChFC programs can be completed through self-study or classroom participation.

Training

Training of salespeople can sometimes be determined by the size and type of firm. Large stock brokerages, such as Edward Jones, A.G. Edwards & Sons and Merrill Lynch, tend to have comprehensive multi-week or month training for salespeople on product knowledge, sales skills and industry rules and regulations. The focus tends to be skewed more towards investments.

Insurance firms vary in their training methods as well. Larger firms tend to have professional training for insurance products and sales skills, but tend to be limited in their training on investment-related products.

Financial-planning firms vary in the training provided. However, better firms usually have

a balanced approach as to the training on investments and insurance products.

In all cases, it's a good idea to inquire:

- How much training did you receive? How much ongoing training do you get?

- Does your office have preferred vendors? (Note: While some internally promoted brands are consistently good performers, others may be promoted because of attached benefits or bonuses.)

Compensation

How a financial professional is compensated depends on his/her firm's parameters and the licenses held by the individual.

1. Commission. Stockbrokers, discount brokers, bank brokers with a Series 7 license and whose firm is properly licensed with the NASD are legally able to charge a commission.

2. Fee for a financial plan. Charging fees requires that both the individual salesperson pass the Series 65 or 66 exams and that his or her firm be licensed as a registered investment adviser. Fees can range from a few hundred to a few thousand dollars. Depending on the firm, some charge a fee for a plan, a retainer fee for annual checkups and, in rare cases, hourly fees. Financial planners or financial advisers most typically offer this arrangement.

3. Asset-based fee. Asset-based fees require that both the individual salesperson pass the Series 65 or 66 exams and that his or her firm be licensed as a registered investment adviser. Financial planners or advisers and some larger stock brokerages offer this choice. These accounts have minimums of $100,000 or higher. The percentage charged drops at various "break points," such as $250,000, $500,000, $1 million, etc.

The key with compensation is that you are comfortable with the compensation and what

POSTSCRIPT

Congratulations for engaging in your first in-depth Money Talk as a couple!! You should be proud of yourselves for showing your commitment to sharing your financial lives together!

And remember: "Life happens," so keep talking and communicating as life challenges you and situations change.

For help with any post-wedding money conversations or planning, I STRONGLY recommend scheduling *annual* review meetings with your financial planner. A good planner will be your go-to person for any decisions relating to your cash flow, regardless of whether they get paid for that purchase/decision.

ENDNOTES

1. John Kenneth Galbraith, renowned economist, *The Age of Uncertainty* (Boston: Houghton Mifflin Harcourt, 1977), Ch. 6.

2. Cheryl D. Broussard, award-winning author of *The Black Woman's Guide to Financial Independence* (1996), "Why Money Is the Leading Cause of Divorce," JET magazine, Nov. 18, 1996.

3. Sara Lawrence-Lightfoot, professor of education, *Worlds Apart* (New York: Basic Books), 1981.

4. Oprah Winfrey, talk show host, television producer, actress, author, & media proprietor, "What I Know For Sure," *O, the Oprah Magazine,* July 2003.

5. Barbara Hall, television writer and producer, *A Summons to New Orleans* (New York: Simon & Schuster, 2000).

6. Plutarch, Greek philosopher, "Of Man's Progress in Virtue," as quoted in *Bartlett's Familiar Quotations*, 10th ed. (Boston: Little, Brown, 1919).

7. Although often attributed to Antoine de Saint-Exupéry, this quote first appeared as an anonymous proverb in *Medical Book of Remedies: 50 Ways to Lose Ten Pounds* (Morton Grove, IL: Publications International, 1995) by Joan Horbiak, founder of Health and Nutrition Network.

ABOUT THE AUTHOR

Nina Needleman, a seasoned financial services professional, specialized in helping couples and families eliminate the tension relating to financial decisions. Her 29 years of experience in the industry was spent helping clients minimize risk and address financial dilemmas. Nina's passion is helping people be good consumers of financial services, so they can obtain the most value in the financial products and services appropriate to their needs.

Her education and credentials include:

- Bachelor of Arts and MBA from Washington University
- Registered Representative (Series 7 & 63)
- Registered Investment Advisory Representative (Series 65)
- Branch Manager and Principal (Series 8 & 24)
- Missouri Life & Health Insurance License
- Dale Carnegie Effective Speaking & Human Relations Course

Since retiring from the business in 2011, Nina has been using her business and financial skills to help nonprofits with Capacity Building and to teach financial literacy and philanthropy. She sees her role now as a Personal Finance Whisperer – helping people ask the right questions to make informed decisions that shape their financial future.

www.ingramcontent.com/pod-product-compliance
Lightning Source LLC
Chambersburg PA
CBHW082111120626
46553CB00011B/3633